Newest titles in the **Explore Your World!** Series

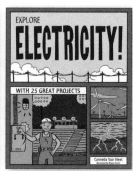
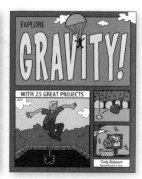

Nomad Press
A division of Nomad Communications
10 9 8 7 6 5 4 3 2 1

This book was manufactured by Sheridan Books,
Ann Arbor, MI USA.
May 2013, Job #346264
ISBN: 978-1-61930-176-4

Illustrations by Bryan Stone
Educational Consultant, Marla Conn

Questions regarding the ordering of this book should be addressed to
Independent Publishers Group
814 N. Franklin St.
Chicago, IL 60610
www.ipgbook.com

Nomad Press
2456 Christian St.
White River Junction, VT 05001
www.nomadpress.net

Nomad Press is committed to preserving ancient forests and natural resources. We elected to print *Explore Flight! with 25 Great Projects* on 2,024 lbs. of Thor PCW containing 30% post consumer waste.

Nomad Press made this paper choice because our printer, Sheridan Books, is a member of Green Press Initiative, a nonprofit program dedicated to supporting authors, publishers, and suppliers in their efforts to reduce their use of fiber obtained from endangered forests.

For more information, visit **www.greenpressinitiative.org**.

Timeline

1000 BCE
* Kites are invented in China.

1200s CE
* The Chinese develop the first rockets.
* Many people attempt to fly using wings or jumping from high places.

1300s
* The Chinese build kites capable of carrying people.

1400s
* Leonardo da Vinci designs a variety of flying machines, including the ornithopter, based on the movement of birds.

1700s
* Joseph and Jacques Montgolfier fly the first hot air balloon.
* Jean Pilatre de Rozier and Marquis d'Arlandes are the first humans to fly in a hot air balloon.
* Andre-Jacques Garnerin makes the first parachute jump.

1800s
* Sir George Cayley builds the first successful glider.
* Henri Giffard flies the first steam engine–powered balloon.
* Otto Lilienthal builds the first practical glider.

1900s
* Count Ferdinand von Zeppelin flies the first of his airships called Zeppelins.
* Orville and Wilbur Wright fly the first powered, heavier-than-air plane.
* Louis Bleriot flies from France to England across the English Channel.

1910s
* Baroness Raymonde de la Roche becomes the first licensed female pilot.
* Airplanes are first used for combat in WWI.
* The U.S. postal service establishes its first airmail route.
* Theodore Roosevelt becomes the first U.S. president to fly in a plane. His flight was after he retired.

1920s
* Bessie Coleman becomes the first licensed African-American pilot.
* Robert Goddard develops the first successful liquid-propelled rocket.
* Charles A. Lindbergh flies nonstop and solo across the Atlantic Ocean.

CONTENTS

Timeline

1930s

* Amelia Earhart becomes the first woman to fly solo across the Atlantic Ocean.
* The first modern helicopter is invented by Igor Sikorsky.
* The golden age of airship travel ends with the *Hindenburg* disaster.
* Frank Whittle invents the jet engine.

1940s

* The Tuskegee airmen play an important role in WWII.
* The Women Airforce Service Pilots (WASPs) formed.
* Captain Chuck Yeager flies faster than the speed of sound.
* Franklin Roosevelt is the first U.S. president in office to travel by plane.

1950s

* Russia launches *Sputnik I*, the first man-made satellite.
* Jet airliners carrying hundreds of passengers begin service.

1960s

* Russian Yuri Gagarin becomes the first person in space.
* Russian Valentina Tereshkova becomes the first woman in space.
* The *Apollo 11* astronauts successfully land on the moon.
* President John F. Kennedy becomes the first U.S. president to fly in his own jet aircraft.

1970s

* The Boeing 747, the largest passenger plane, begins service across the Atlantic Ocean.
* The U.S. launches its first space station, called *Skylab*, proving people can live in space for extended periods of time.
* The first supersonic passenger airliner, the Concorde, begins service.

1980s

* The first Space Shuttle, *Columbia*, is launched.
* Sally Ride becomes the first American woman in space.
* Jeana Yeager and Dick Rutan pilot the airplane *Voyager*, becoming the first to circle the world without refueling.

1990s

* Steve Fossett becomes the first person to fly a balloon solo around the world.
* 11-year-old Victoria van Meter becomes the youngest girl to fly solo across America.

2000s

* *SpaceShipOne* becomes the first privately manned spacecraft.
* Construction on the largest orbiting laboratory, the *International Space Station*, is completed.

v

Let's Explore Flight!

Have you ever wanted to soar like a bird? Have you imagined what it would be like to race through the sky like a superhero? Well, for thousands of years, people just like you have wanted to fly above the land and sea.

● ●

Some tried flapping their arms. Others made wings of feathers and parachutes of cloth. There were dreamers who sketched designs of amazing-looking flying machines and those who experimented with kites, balloons, and **gliders**. And in the last 100 years there were inventors who built aircraft powered by engines.

1

EXPLORE FLIGHT!

What is flight? How do airplanes fly? Who were the first people to build flying machines? In this book you'll explore how things fly and the exciting history of flight—from kites in 500 **BCE** to present-day spacecraft.

Explore Flight! will answer many of your questions. You'll meet amazing people like the Montgolfier brothers, Otto Lilienthal, Charles Lindbergh, and Elizabeth "Bessie" Coleman. You'll learn about **aeronauts**, record breakers, and inventors and read **myths** and **legends** about flight from around the world.

The fun experiments and projects in this book will help you understand the science behind flight. For example, why birds can fly but we can't. You'll come across lots of silly jokes and fun facts too. Don't be surprised if by the end of this book you know the basic parts of a plane, can send a message using the **aviator's** alphabet, and have made your own flying machine.

What are you waiting for? Jump into the cockpit and lower your flight goggles. Let's Explore Flight!

WORDS TO KNOW!

glider: an aircraft that can fly without an engine by riding air currents. It is towed up by an aircraft with an engine.

BCE: put after a date, BCE stands for Before Common Era and counts down to zero. CE stands for Common Era and counts up from zero. These non-religious terms correspond to BC and AD.

aeronaut: a traveler in a flying craft.

myth: a story about make-believe creatures that people once believed were real.

legend: a story about heroes from the past.

aviator: a pilot.

2

THE HISTORY OF FLIGHT

When people talk about the history of flight, they are talking about events that happened over a long period of time. Since the creation of kites around 500 BCE, more than 2,000 years passed before the Wright Brothers first invented powered flight in 1903 CE. A little more than 50 years later, the first modern spacecraft was launched into space.

WORDS TO KNOW!

glide: to come in for a landing and to land without using engine power. Also, to move smoothly and effortlessly through the air or the water.

But have you ever stopped to think about flight in the natural world? The history of natural flight is millions of years old!

First there were leaves and seeds. Leaves and seeds may not have wings like a bird, but they can travel. They hitch a ride on the wind. Some seed structures twirl like a helicopter. Others float through the air on fine hairs that act as a parachute. Some **glide**. The football-sized seed pod of the Indonesian Alsomitra vine produces gliding seeds with wings up to 6 inches across (15 centimeters)!

HOW DO THINGS FLY?

Before we dive into the fun activities in this book, we are going to look at four **forces** that affect flight. A force is a push or a pull that moves an object. You push a friend on a swing. You pull on your socks in the morning.

Lift, **gravity**, **thrust**, and **drag** are the basic forces acting on all flying objects. Forces always act in pairs. Lift pushes the airplane up. A plane's wings and its movement through the air create lift. Gravity pulls downward on the airplane. Thrust moves the plane forward. Propellers and jet engines provide airplanes with thrust. The fourth force, drag, slows the plane down.

WORDS TO KNOW!

force: a push or a pull.

lift: an upward force.

gravity: the pull of all objects toward the center of the earth.

thrust: a force that pushes an object forward.

drag: the force pushing against an object as it moves through the air.

In order for any object to stay in the air, all four forces have to be in balance.

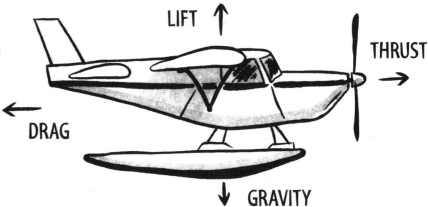

4

There's a tug-of-war going on all the time between lift and gravity, and between thrust and drag. If one force is stronger than the other, the plane won't be stable. Throughout this book you will read more about these four forces and how flying machines are perfectly designed to stay up in the air.

ANIMALS THAT FLY

WORDS TO KNOW!

reptile: an animal covered with scales that crawls on its belly or on short legs. Snakes, turtles, and alligators are reptiles.

Triassic Period: 250 to 200 million years ago.

Cretaceous Period: 144 to 65 million years ago.

Scientists believe that insects began to fly about 360 million years ago. Massive flying **reptiles** called Pterosaurs, some with wingspans of 40 feet (12 meters), ruled the skies from the end of the **Triassic Period** to the end of the **Cretaceous Period**. Birds and bats followed.

Today, insects, bats, and birds are the only animals on Earth that can fly. They all have wings to lift them up and keep them moving through the air. These animals don't have engines like airplanes to provide thrust. Instead they rely on their own energy to take off and fly.

Some animals, including flying squirrels, snakes, fish, and frogs, can glide. The Wallace flying frog can glide over 50 feet (15 meters) from tree to tree. When it jumps, it spreads out membranes between its toes that act like a parachute so it falls more slowly.

DID YOU KNOW?

Insects are the largest group of flying creatures. Their wings don't beat up and down like the wings of birds or bats. They actually form a figure eight to create lift. While insects like dragonflies may look delicate, their strong wings allow them to **hover** like a helicopter. And some **species** of dragonflies can fly as fast as 20 miles per hour (32 kilometers)!

Birds are strong too. Wouldn't it be fun to fly at the speed of a racecar, like the peregrine falcon? This falcon is the fastest bird on Earth in its hunting dive, reaching speeds of over 200 miles per hour (321 kilometers). Birds are able to fly because they have powerful chest muscles to beat their wings up, down, and forward. As birds beat their wings, air moves over the wings faster than it does below them because bird wings are curved on top. This creates more **air pressure** below the wing, which pushes the wing up.

For thousands of years people dreamed of flying like birds. Today, over 4 million people fly on planes every day, all around the world.

DID YOU KNOW?

Bats can't fly as fast as peregrine falcons, but they are record setters. A bat is the only flying **mammal**. Plus, they have the fastest mammal muscles, capable of beating their wings up to 200 times per second! Unlike birds that have feathers, bat wings are made of skin, bone, and muscle.

Isn't natural flight amazing! No wonder people have studied flying creatures for thousands of years. Some of our **ancestors** tried to copy bird flight. Let's find out if they were successful.

WORDS TO KNOW!

mammal: a group of animals that includes humans, dogs, and mice. These animals have backbones, feed their young with milk, and are mostly covered with hair.

ancestor: a person who lived before you.

engineer: someone who uses science and math to design and build things.

JUST FOR LAUGHS

Why do geese fly south in the winter?
Because it's too far to walk!

INSPIRED INVENTION

The **engineers** at Lockheed Martin are developing a machine that flies like a maple tree seed. Their Unmanned Aerial Vehicle (UAV), called the Samurai, spins around and around to achieve lift. Equipped with a camera, the Samurai may be used in the future for military missions.

7

Flying Seeds and Leaves

In autumn it's possible to watch as spinning seeds and gliding leaves drop from trees. In this activity you will discover which seeds and leaves are near your home.

1 Search for leaves and seeds on the ground in your own backyard, or at a nearby park or trail with a grownup. Try to find as many different examples as possible.

2 Place the seeds and leaves carefully into a plastic container.

3 At home, spread your examples out on a flat, dry surface.

4 Examine the seeds and leaves with a magnifying glass and write down your observations.

5 Sort and group the leaves and seeds based on color, texture, shape, and size.

6 Next, create a chart from your data by writing your sorting ideas along the top of the paper. Use a ruler to divide the sections.

7 Glue one example of each seed and leaf into the correct section. Save the rest for the next activity.

THINGS TO THINK ABOUT: Were the seeds or leaves all the same size? Did more seeds have wings or hairs?

Air Resistance Experiment

Air resistance, or drag, pushes against all objects as they fall. In this activity you'll observe how air resistance affects seeds, leaves, and household objects as they travel through the air.

1 Hold your objects slightly above eye level and drop them one by one.

2 Watch how quickly or slowly the objects reach the ground. Record your observations in a notebook.

3 Next, stand on top of a picnic table or chair and hold a different object in each hand. Before you drop the objects, predict which one will reach the ground first. Record your results in a notebook.

SUPPLIES

- assorted seeds and leaves
- crumbled up sheet of paper
- feather
- sheet of tissue paper
- magazine
- notebook
- pencil
- chair

THINGS TO THINK ABOUT: How do you think the shape of an object affects its flight? Do movements of any objects in this experiment remind you of a flying machine?

WHAT'S HAPPENING? Air resistance is drag. It slows down everything that moves in the air. One way that airplane engineers reduce air resistance is by designing a streamlined vehicle. A streamlined vehicle has a smooth shape. A smooth shape lets air move freely over the aircraft's surface.

Dreaming of Flight

Look into the sky and you just might see a plane soar overhead. Imagine explaining that to someone who lived thousands of years ago when flight was only for the birds or, in some cases, the gods.

• •

Kids have always loved listening to myths and legends about a flying carpet, airborne chariot, or winged horse. While these flying machines and beasts sound amazing in stories, they aren't real. But long ago, people believed they were.

Dreaming of Flight

A myth from 1500 BCE tells of a Persian king who flew on a throne carried by four eagles. England also had a flying ruler. King Bladud is said to have used magic to make himself a pair of wings. While attempting to fly, his magical wings failed him and he fell to his death.

The ancient Greeks had many flying stories. The god Apollo is said to have driven his sun chariot across the sky, which explained why there was day and night. And the flying horse Pegasus inspired people with his adventures.

One of the most famous myths tells of Daedalus and Icarus. Daedalus, a great inventor, and his son Icarus were imprisoned on the island of Crete. Daedalus built wings of feathers and wax so they could escape. Daedalus warned his son that the wax would melt if he flew too close to the sun, but Icarus didn't listen. He flew so high that his wings melted and he fell into the sea.

Around 500 BCE, the ancient Chinese began flying kites. Some kites were for play but others were so large they could lift a soldier into the air to spy on an enemy.

DID YOU KNOW?

In China there's a legend of a great archer who received a magical potion. Before he could drink it, his wife drank it all! She began to feel lighter and lighter, until she floated to the moon. It is said that if you look up at the moon, you may see her there in her Moon Palace.

TRYING TO FLY

People have always wanted to fly. Abbas Ibn Firnas was an inventor and aviator in Spain. He is thought to have been one of the first people to make a flying machine. In the ninth **century** he jumped from a tower in Spain with a wooden glider covered in feathers. According to reports, he flew a short distance and badly injured himself when he landed. But this didn't stop the tower jumpers of the **Medieval Era**. They tried to fly by jumping from a high place and flapping their wing-like inventions. All of these attempts failed and often ended in tragic deaths.

WORDS TO KNOW!

century: a period of 100 years.

Medieval Era: A period of time between the fall of the Roman Empire and the Renaissance, roughly between 350 and 1450 CE. Also known as the Middle Ages.

Then & Now

Then: People tried flapping their arms to fly. They did not understand that humans are simply not built to fly.

Now: We know that the only way people can fly is with a machine that will lift them off the ground.

It took centuries for people to understand **aeronautics**. During the fifteenth century, Italian scientist, inventor, and artist Leonardo da Vinci spent years recording the movements of birds. He understood that birds' flapping wings made them fly. He knew that air passing over their wings created lift.

So why couldn't he build a machine to do the same thing? In 1485, Leonardo designed a wing-flapping aircraft called an ornithopter. It relied on human strength for power. But since Leonardo never actually built his ornithopter, he didn't realize it was too heavy to work.

JUST FOR LAUGHS

Why were the pilot's arms tired?
He had just flown in!

It took all the way until 2010 before anyone successfully flew an ornithopter. Students from the University of Toronto made **aviation** history when they designed and flew an ornithopter a distance of 475 feet (145 meters).

Ornithopter

Throughout history people have designed ornithopters using different types of materials. In this activity, you are going to make a miniature version that will soar thanks to a rubber band **catapult**. Make sure an adult is present when you launch your ornithopter.

1 Open the card. Draw a large curved banana shape on the card for the wings and a smaller one for the fin of your ornithopter. Cut the shapes out with scissors.

2 Glue craft feathers to the top of the wing. You don't want to glue too many or your ornithopter will be too heavy to glide.

3 Use clear tape to attach the wings to the craft stick body roughly one-third down from one end. Attach the fin to the other end with tape. Bend the edges up slightly.

WORDS TO KNOW!

catapult: a mechanical device that launches a glider or aircraft.

14

DID YOU KNOW?

4 Thread the rubber band through the paper clip. Secure the paper clip with masking tape to the underside of your ornithopter where the wings are attached.

5 Insert the pencil into the free end of the rubber band. Hold your ornithopter at arm's length away from you and pull the elastic towards you with the pencil. Do not point your ornithopter at a person or an animal. Make sure the coast is clear and let go!

THINGS TO TRY: Use different materials, such as tissue paper or cloth, for the wings.

JUST FOR LAUGHS

What do you call a fly with no wings?
A walk!

Kite

You're going to make a diamond-shaped kite. Use it on a clear, windy day, away from power lines.

- piece of paper, 8.5 by 11 inches (216 x 279 millimeters)
- scissors
- clear tape
- colored pencils, markers
- twig or drinking straw
- long string or yarn
- pencil
- tissue paper

1 Take your paper and make it a square. Do this by folding up the bottom left corner until the bottom edge of the paper meets flush with the right edge of the paper. You'll have a triangle and about 3 inches of paper showing at the top (7½ centimeters). Cut off the top strip of paper where it meets the triangle.

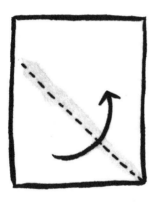

2 Unfold the paper and place it on a flat surface. Rotate the sheet until it looks like a diamond.

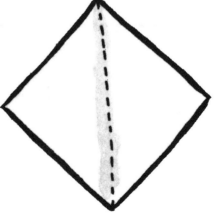

3 Fold the right and left corners of the paper into the middle crease. The entire bottom right and bottom left edges should line up with this middle crease. Press down firmly. Secure these edges together with tape.

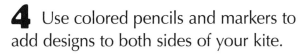

4 Use colored pencils and markers to add designs to both sides of your kite.

5 Tape a skinny twig or a straw across the kite at the top of the back fold.

6 Tie one end of the string around the center of the twig and make a knot. Tape it down to keep it in place.

7 Tape the other end of the string to a pencil and wind up the string.

8 Add tissue paper streamers, 2 to 3 feet long (60 to 91 centimeters), to the bottom of the kite.

9 Wait for a windy day and see how long you can keep your kite in the air!

THINGS TO TRY: Make the streamers longer. Make your kite larger or smaller. Experiment with different kite shapes and observe how they fly.

WHAT'S HAPPENING? A kite will stay in the air as long as the force lifting it into the air is stronger than gravity. Kite fliers try to lean a kite into the wind to keep the kite flying. This is called the angle of attack.

Phenakistoscope

Leonardo da Vinci studied bird flight to learn how a person might take flight. Create a phenakistoscope movie of a bird in flight. The phenakistoscope was invented before there were movies to make things look like they're in motion.

1 Cut a file folder in half. With your compass, draw a large circle on one half.

2 Cut the circle out with your scissors.

3 Divide the circle into even sections using the pencil compass. You could also divide it by folding the circle lightly in half, in half again, and then in half once more. This will make 8 sections.

4 Cut small slits around the edge on both sides of the sections.

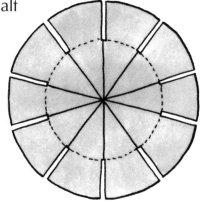

5 In each section draw an image of a bird in a different stage of flight. Look online with an adult for ideas, or look in a book.

6 Push the pencil through the center of the circle so the eraser sticks out the front side with the images.

7 Stand in front of a mirror with the images on the phenakistoscope facing the mirror.

8 Hold the phenakistoscope from the back, in front of your face. Spin the phenakistoscope using the pencil. Look through the slits at the images as it spins. Can you see the bird moving?

Flying Myth

A myth is a story about an imaginary creature. Imagine you're a storyteller living in a time before people had built flying machines. What kind of flying myth would you create to express your desire to fly?

SUPPLIES

- notebook
- pencil

1 Use these questions to get started:

- Where does your story take place?

- Who is the hero or heroine and what makes this person special?

- Are there other characters in the story?

- Who are the imaginary creatures? Can they talk? What is special about them?

- What is the story problem and how is it solved?

2 Write down the key ideas and events of your myth and then practice telling your story out loud. When you're ready, share the flying myth with your friends and family!

INSPIRED INVENTION

The Nano Hummingbird is a tiny, remote-controlled flying machine that can hover and fly forward and backward. Equipped with a camera, it might be used by the police and military in the future.

Up, Up, and Away

The curious French brothers Joseph and Jacques Montgolfier wondered what made the smoke in their fireplace rise up the chimney. To find out, they lit a fire under the opening of a silk bag. It rose up too. The brothers believed that fire created a special gas that made the bag rise. They called this Montgolfier gas. In fact, this gas was simply warm air. What the brothers discovered, without understanding it, is that warm air weighs less than cool air. So an object filled with warm air will rise.

• •

Eventually, the brothers' curiosity led to the launch of the first hot air balloon on June 4, 1783. They burned straw and wool under their balloon and watched it rise 3,000 feet high (1,000 meters) before landing over a mile away (over 1½ kilometers).

Up, Up, and Away

After more experiments with small balloons, the brothers were ready to build a balloon big enough to carry people. They came close on September 19, 1783, when they launched an elaborate balloon in front of 130,000 people at the **Palace of Versailles**. With the king watching through a telescope from his apartment, the balloon flew nearly 2 miles (3 kilometers) before returning to the ground with the passengers safe and sound. Who were these lucky passengers? A sheep, a rooster, and a duck!

WORDS TO KNOW!

Palace of Versailles: the home of the French royal family who ruled from 1682 to 1789.

A month later, the Montgolfiers constructed a beautiful blue and gold balloon 70 feet tall (21 meters) and 49 feet across (12 meters). Now who would be the brave aeronaut? King Louis XVI wanted it to be a prisoner, but he agreed to let the scientist Jean François Pilatre de Rozier and the Marquis d'Arlandes have the honor. On November 21, 1783, the balloon sailed for 5 miles (8 kilometers) and landed 25 minutes later, making these men the first humans to travel in a hot air balloon.

JUST FOR LAUGHS

What did the sheep say when asked to fly?
This is a baaaaaad idea.

WORDS TO KNOW!

pioneer: to be the first to do or discover something.

English Channel: an arm of the Atlantic Ocean separating England from France.

prototype: a working model.

American Civil War: a war fought from 1861 to 1865 between the 11 states that formed the Confederacy and the 25 Union states supported by the federal government.

Drawn by the magic of flight, more **pioneering** balloonists like Jean-Pierre Blanchard worked on balloons. Blanchard crossed the **English Channel** by balloon in 1785 and made the first balloon flight in North America in 1793. American James Jackson Pennington's *Aerial Bird* used a fan to draw in air and inflate it. He never had enough money to build a full-scale **prototype**, so his wife sold his design to the Wright brothers for $500.

SPY BALLOONS IN AMERICA

Hot air balloons found an important purpose during the **American Civil War**. The Union army from the north and Confederate army from the south used hot air balloons to spy on each other.

Thaddeus Lowe, a famous balloonist, convinced President Lincoln that hot air balloons made good spying machines. President Lincoln agreed and soon the Union had a Balloon Corps. After Lowe successfully spied on Confederate soldiers, he built six more balloons for the Balloon Corps. But these spy missions were expensive, and in 1863, the Balloon Corps shut down.

AIRSHIPS

Maybe you've heard of a blimp. But have you ever heard of a dirigible? In 1852, French engineer Henri Jacques Giffard invented the dirigible, known as a blimp. Unlike a hot air balloon, a dirigible could be steered and had power. The dirigible was a big envelope shaped like a hot dog. When filled with lightweight **hydrogen** gas, it could rise in the heavier air.

An open basket called a gondola hung underneath to hold people. The pilot steered with a **rudder** attached to the basket, and a **steam engine** powered a propeller at the back. A horse and carriage could easily outrun a dirigible traveling at 3 miles per hour (5 kilometers).

WORDS TO KNOW!

hydrogen: a gas that is lighter than air.

rudder: a fin-like device used to steer a vehicle through water or air.

steam engine: an engine powered by steam, first invented by James Watt in 1775.

Today, blimps like the Goodyear Blimp are filled with helium gas instead of hydrogen gas, because hydrogen gas can burn or explode.

 **DID YOU KNOW?**

WORDS TO KNOW!

technology: tools, methods, or systems used to solve a problem or do work.

commercial: operating as a business to earn money.

Airship **technology** got better and better over the next 50 years. Lighter and more powerful engines replaced the steam engine. In 1900, a German count named Ferdinand von Zeppelin launched the biggest airship the world had ever seen. A Zeppelin looked like a blimp with hard sides, but it was bigger and could carry more weight. Before **commercial** passenger airplanes, Zeppelins were a popular way for travelers to fly between Europe and America.

In 1936, the largest and most comfortable Zeppelin ever built began service. Called the *Hindenburg*, it was longer than two football fields! For a $400 one-way ticket, passengers could enjoy the *Hindenburg's* dining

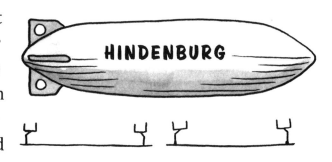

room, a piano lounge, and a great view of the land below. That's like spending $6,500 for a one-way ticket today. Four huge diesel engines powered the *Hindenburg*, which transported 70 passengers from Frankfurt, Germany, to Lakehurst, New Jersey, in 60 hours.

JUST FOR LAUGHS

Why did the rooster ride in the hot air balloon?
Because he wasn't a chicken!

Tragically, on May 6, 1937, the *Hindenburg* burst into flames just as it was preparing to land in New Jersey. The explosion killed 36 people. This accident put an end to lighter-than-air ships.

THE PARACHUTE

Over the past few hundred years, people have used cloaks, hats, and pieces of fabric to slow down falls from great heights. It took Frenchman Louis-Sébastien Lenormand many jumps from low heights using umbrellas until, in 1783, he constructed a cone-shaped canopy from cloth. After a successful jump from a tower with his cloth, Lenormand was credited with creating the word parachute. *Para* comes from the Greek meaning to prevent and *chute* comes from the French for fall. So parachute means "prevent the fall."

Two years later, hot air balloon pioneer Jean-Pierre Blanchard switched to parachutes. He carried out experiments with small animals, like a dog and a squirrel. Luckily for the animals, the tests were a success. In 1797, another man named André-Jacques Garnerin became the first person to successfully parachute from a balloon.

In July 2000, skydiver Adrian Nicholas tested a model of a parachute sketched by Leonardo da Vinci in 1483. Nicholas jumped from a hot air balloon at 9,842 feet (3,000 meters) and floated for roughly 10 minutes before cutting himself free. He used a modern parachute to return safely to the ground.

DID YOU KNOW?

What did these early parachutes look like? Before the 1700s, parachutes were wooden frames covered in cloth. They looked like open umbrellas. By the end of the 1700s, parachutes were lighter, stronger, flexible, and made of silk. During **World War I** and **World War II**, pilots and soldiers jumped from planes using parachutes that were small enough to fit in backpacks.

Today, parachutes are used in many ways. Skydivers who jump for fun use them to slow their descent. The military uses them to drop **cargo**, people, and medical supplies from planes and helicopters. **NASA** (National Aeronautics and Space Administration) used a 70-foot-wide parachute in 2012 (21 meters) to help land its rover *Curiosity* on Mars.

INSPIRED INVENTION

The Sherpa is a GPS-supported, remote-controlled parachute used by the United States military and Special Forces. It delivers cargo and helps with search and rescue. Some versions of the Sherpa can safely deliver up to 10,000 pounds of cargo to the ground (4,536 kilograms).

Blimp

Goodyear Blimps are a common sight at sporting events. But you don't have to wait for a major game to see a blimp. Now you can make your own. Do this activity inside so your blimp doesn't float away.

SUPPLIES

- 6 feet of ribbon or string (1.8 meters)
- scissors
- 2 helium balloons
- egg carton
- ruler
- colored markers
- pennies or other small weights

1 Cut the ribbon in half. Tie a piece of ribbon to the bottom of each helium balloon. Tie the balloons to a doorknob while you work on the rest of the craft.

2 Make the gondola by cutting three egg holders from an egg carton. Decorate the gondola with colored markers.

3 Make a hole on either end of the gondola for your ribbon to fit through. Thread the ribbon through the holes so that the distance between the balloons and the gondola is roughly 16 inches (40 centimeters) and knot them securely. Both balloons need to be the same height.

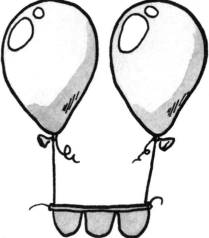

4 Let go of your blimp inside and watch what happens.

5 Add pennies to the egg holders and observe what happens with the added weight.

WHAT'S HAPPENING? Your blimp floats because helium is lighter than air. The pennies represent bags, called ballonets, used on real airships. Ballonets are filled with air. When the ballonets are emptied, the airship goes up. When the ballonets are filled, the airship slowly comes down.

Da Vinci Parachute

Parachutes are used for fun and to transport medical supplies, food, water, and people to areas where planes and helicopters can't land.

1 Draw a 3½-inch line on the paper (9 centimeters). Then use the protractor to measure 60-degree angles at each end. Draw lines 3½ inches long and connect them to form an equilateral triangle.

2 Repeat this three more times. Cut out all four equilateral triangles and use your markers or crayons to decorate them.

SUPPLIES

- paper
- ruler
- pencil
- protractor
- scissors
- crayons/markers
- clear tape
- dental floss
- a small weight such as an action figure

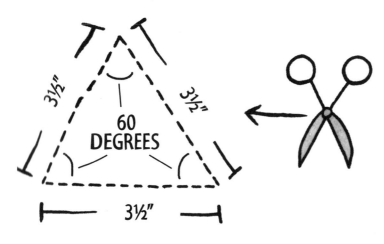

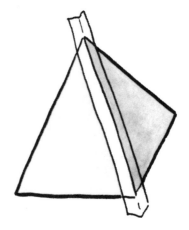

3 Using clear tape, attach all four triangles to each other to create a pyramid.

4 Make a small hole with the scissors at the bottom of each of the four triangles. Make one small hole at the tip of the pyramid.

 28

5 Cut four pieces of dental floss 8 inches long (20 centimeters), and one piece 12 inches long (30 centimeters).

6 Thread the 12-inch floss through the top of the pyramid and knot it at the top. It should hang down. Attach the smaller floss strings to the other holes. Tie all five strings together.

7 Attach your small weight to the end of the 12-inch piece of floss.

8 Test your parachute by dropping it from various heights.

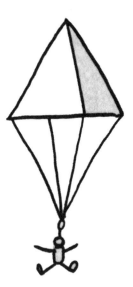

THINGS TO TRY: Use a stopwatch to record how long it takes the parachute to land. Change the weight at the end of the floss to a bolt or a paperclip, or anything else you would like to try. Shorten or lengthen the strings. Make the parachute out of different materials. Try a variety of shapes and sizes of parachutes.

WHAT'S HAPPENING? A parachute works by creating a form of resistance called drag. As the parachute opens up, it becomes filled with air, slowing the rate of fall.

Then & Now

Then: Around 2200 BCE, Chinese emperor Shin is said to have jumped from a high tower with two large hats acting as parachutes.

Now: Skydivers jump from heights of 13,000 feet (4,000 meters) using square or rectangular parachutes made of lightweight nylon.

Mini Hot Air Balloon

From the eighteenth to the mid-nineteenth century, people did not know how to control a hot air balloon. The balloon simply traveled wherever the wind took it. Use a hair dryer to heat the air in your own hot air balloon and see what happens. **Please have an adult present when you use the hair dryer.**

SUPPLIES

- 1 large paper cupcake liner
- crayons or colored pencils
- scissors
- thread
- clear tape
- small cellophane bag about 5 x 11 inches (3 x 28 centimeters)
- hair dryer

1 Decorate your cupcake liner with crayons or colored pencils and set it aside.

2 Cut four pieces of thread 6 inches in length (15 centimeters). Tape the end of one piece of thread inside each open corner of the cellophane bag. Tape the other ends of the thread to the cupcake liner.

3 Put your hair dryer on a low setting and aim the nozzle at the opening of the bag. Observe what happens as the bag fills with air from the hair dryer.

THINGS TO THINK ABOUT: Did your bag take off? Why or why not? Would this experiment work if there were holes in the bag? Why or why not?

WHAT'S HAPPENING? Air is made up of tiny molecules. When air heats up, the molecules spread apart, which makes the air lighter. As the air in the bag heats up it becomes lighter than the air around it, so the bag is lifted up.

 30

People Can Fly!

Do you like making paper airplanes or flying kites? Both are simple types of gliders. A glider is any aircraft without an engine. Hang gliders, sailplanes, and even the Space Shuttle as it returns to Earth are also gliders. What keeps gliders in the air? The force of lift produced by their wings. The faster the speed of a glider, the more lift its wings make.

● ●

British engineer Sir George Cayley was a glider pioneer. He was the first person to understand that the forces of gravity, lift, drag, and thrust kept birds gliding without needing to flap their wings.

WORDS TO KNOW!

WORDS TO KNOW!

hang glider: a piloted aircraft made of cloth that looks like a parachute or big kite.

sailplane: a piloted glider with aircraft parts, construction, and flight control systems, but no engine.

anatomy: the structure of a living thing.

In 1809, Cayley built a glider that lifted a 10-year-old child off the ground for a few yards. By 1853, at the age of 80, he was ready to test a full-sized glider. Cayley didn't want to fly the machine, so his coachman John Appleby became the first person in the world to successfully fly in a fixed-wing glider. Appleby immediately quit his job, saying that he had not been hired to fly!

In 1891, Otto Lilienthal built the first useful glider. Bird flight fascinated Lilienthal. As a young boy in Germany, he spent hours studying birds and wing **anatomy**. He finally discovered how birds flapped their wings to create lift and thrust. Lilienthal was sure that with large enough wings, he could fly too.

In 1889, he came up with tables that calculated the amount of lift based on a wing's size and shape. He published his findings in a book, *Birdflight as the Basis for Aviation*. Future glider builders, including the Wright brothers, studied his book.

Lilienthal built 16 different gliders using willow wood and waxed cotton. By strapping himself to his glider, waiting for a good wind, and then running down a hill, Lilienthal would soar into the sky. Crowds of people watched his flights, and photographs of the "Flying Man" spread from Europe to America.

After 2,000 safe flights, August 9, 1896, was Lilienthal's last. He died after a strong wind pushed the nose of his glider up and he fell 50 feet to the ground (15 meters).

POWERED FLIGHT

Gliders could fly but not for long enough. Inventors in the mid-1800s tried to solve this by powering flying machines with steam engines. A steam engine's energy came from coal or wood burned in its boiler.

One attempt was William Henson and John Stringfellow's Aerial Steam Carriage. The men printed brochures showing their invention flying over the Egyptian pyramids before ever conducting a single test. When Henson and Stringfellow did make a model, it never took flight. Their steam-powered engine was just not powerful enough.

THE FIRST AIRPLANES

Crashes didn't stop inventors from working to improve flying machines. American Samuel Pierpont Langley was a pioneer in aeronautics research. In 1887 he began building an unmanned flying machine. It had **tandem wings** and two propellers powered by a steam engine. Langley called his model flyer an Aerodrome, meaning air runner in Greek.

In 1895, Langley's Aerodrome No.5 was ready. The Aerodrome was catapulted into the air off a houseboat on the Potomac River. It flew over 3,000 feet into the air (1,000 meters), making the world's first successful flight of an unpiloted, engine-driven, heavier-than-air craft of substantial size. President McKinley gave Langley $50,000 to build an Aerodrome that could carry a person.

In 1903, after many changes to his design, Langley was ready. Unfortunately, two test flights of his piloted Great Aerodrome crashed into the river. Luckily, the pilot swam to safety both times.

34

INSPIRED INVENTION

The military uses gliders to deliver cargo quietly to ground personnel. The Hawkeye is a tandem-wing glider that can be piloted by remote control for up to 50 miles (80 kilometers).

THE WRIGHT BROTHERS

While Langley was busy with his invention, two brothers were working on their own piloted flying machines. And in December 1903, only nine days after Langley's failure, Wilbur and Orville Wright succeeded.

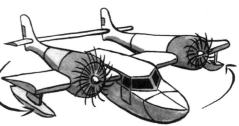

PITCH

These bike builders from Dayton, Ohio, were fascinated by flight as children. They played endlessly with their toy helicopter, the Penaud flying screw. As adults they read everything they could on flight.

ROLL

The brothers chose Kitty Hawk, North Carolina, a place with a steady breeze, to experiment with their kites and gliders. After hundreds of tests, the Wrights understood they needed to control their aircraft in three directions. An airplane can fall or climb (pitch), tilt to the right or left (roll), and turn right or left (yaw).

YAW

WORDS TO KNOW!

biplane: a plane with two pairs of wings, one above the other.

aerodynamic: having a shape that reduces the amount of drag on something when it moves through the air.

anemometer: a device used to measure wind speed.

The Wrights built a wind tunnel where they conducted over 200 tests of their model wings. They were finally ready to fly their Wright Flyer I, the first gas-powered airplane. Flyer I was a **biplane** made from lightweight birch wood. It had a four-cylinder engine and many **aerodynamic** features, including two 8-foot-wide propellers (244 centimeters).

From his position lying down on the bottom wing, the pilot controlled pulleys and cables attached to the wings. He twisted the tips of the wings in opposite directions to keep the plane from rolling. An **anemometer** was onboard to measure wind speeds. Using wind speeds and a stopwatch, the pilot could calculate his airspeed. On December 17, 1903, Wilbur flew 852 feet (260 meters) in the Wright Flyer I in 59 seconds! After years of experimenting and testing, the Wrights became the first people in history to fly an airplane.

JUST FOR LAUGHS

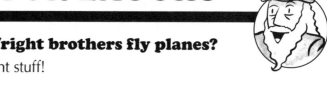

Why did the Wright brothers fly planes?
They had the Wright stuff!

FLYING TAKES OFF!

After the Wright brothers' success, advances in aviation came quickly. In August 1909, aviators gathered in France to compete for prizes. The contest was a huge success. Records were set for **altitude**, speed, and distance. American builder and pilot Glenn H. Curtiss won a trophy for having the fastest time in a 12-mile air race (20 kilometer). Newspapers declared him "Champion Aviator of the World."

WORDS TO KNOW!

altitude: height above sea level.

box-kite airplane: a kite with an engine and a tail added.

monoplane: an airplane with one set of wings.

Just the month before, a London newspaper offered a cash prize to the first pilot to fly across the English Channel between France and England. Inventor and aircraft designer Louis Bleriot had been experimenting with ornithopters, gliders, and **box-kite airplanes**. His **monoplane** had flown for 20 minutes. He decided to take a chance. On July 25, 1909, he made it 22 miles across the Channel (35 kilometers) and collected his money!

Bleriot became an instant celebrity. He formed a plane manufacturing company that built the first planes ever used in war. They were used early in World War I for spying and by the end of the war as fighter planes.

Glider

Gliders come in all shapes and sizes, but they all need wings to fly.

1 Place a small amount of clay on the sharp end of the bamboo skewer.

2 Cut the paper in half lengthwise. Fold the short sides of one piece together so the paper is folded in half. Make a mark along the fold 4 inches up (10 centimeters). Make a mark along the opposite edge 1½ inches up (4 centimeters). Use your ruler to join the points together.

3 Cut along the line and unfold the paper to reveal the wings for your glider.

4 From a scrap piece of paper, make the tail the same shape as the wing but half the size. Also cut out a small triangle for the fin.

5 Tape the wing piece to the skewer about 2 inches from the clay tip (5 centimeters). Tape the tail to the other end of the skewer. The edge of the tail and the end of the bamboo skewer should line up. Tape the fin to the center of the tail so it sticks up into the air.

6 Hold the glider in one hand above your head, aim the nose up, and launch it into the air.

THINGS TO TRY: Design a glider with shorter or longer wings or wings with different shapes. Add weight, like a paperclip, to your glider. Experiment with different places to attach the weight.

SUPPLIES

- 9-inch bamboo skewer (25 centimeters)
- clay
- printer paper
- pencil
- ruler
- scissors
- clear tape

 38

Thrust and Drag

Ride your bicycle on a windy day to discover how wind can make your ride easier or harder.

SUPPLIES

- bicycle
- stopwatch or a watch with a second hand
- windy day
- paper and pencil

1 Mark off a distance of about 100 yards, or about the length of a football field, where you can ride your bike.

2 Ask a friend to time you as you try to cycle into the wind. Notice how hard you have to pedal. Do you feel air pushing against you? This is drag. Record your time.

3 Now ask a friend to time you as you cycle with the wind behind you. Go the same distance you biked before. Notice how the wind pushes you along. This is thrust. Write down your time and distance. How does it compare with your first time?

WHAT'S HAPPENING? When you biked into the wind, it pushed against you. This is drag, a force that works against forward motion. When cyclists race, they use bicycles and helmets that are aerodynamic and wear tight bike suits to cut down on drag.

Airfoil

An airplane wing has a special shape called an airfoil. The top of the wing curves more than the bottom. Air moves faster over the top and slower underneath. The Bernoulli Effect explains that the faster air moves, the less pressure it applies. So there is more pressure from the slow-moving air under the wings, which pushes the plane up. **Please have an adult present when you use the hair dryer.**

SUPPLIES

- 1 piece of paper
- ruler
- pencil
- scissors
- tape
- ribbon
- cereal box
- 2 bamboo skewers or straws
- hair dryer

1 Cut a strip of paper about 1½ inches wide by 8 inches long (4 by 20 centimeters). Fold the short sides together without making a crease and tape the ends flat.

2 Cut two 8-inch lengths of ribbon (20 centimeters) and tape one in the middle of the airfoil near the top curve and the other in the same spot on the underside of the airfoil.

3 To construct your air tunnel, open up one end of a cereal box. Stand the box upright and tape it to a counter top.

4 Poke two holes, roughly 2 inches apart (5 centimeters) and directly across from each other in the middle of each large side of the open box. Insert the bamboo skewers through the holes, all the way through the box.

DID YOU KNOW?

5 Hang your airfoil from the skewers on the outside of the tunnel on either side so that it is level.

6 Put your hair dryer on a low setting. Aim it at the curved edge of the airfoil, and watch what happens to the ribbons.

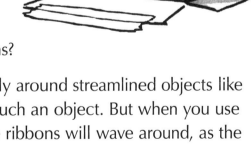

THINGS TO TRY: Try designing airfoils in different shapes. Try using objects that are not streamlined such as square- or rectangular-shaped objects. What happens to the ribbons?

WHAT'S HAPPENING? Air travels easily around streamlined objects like airfoils. The ribbons will blow over such an object. But when you use an object that is not streamlined, the ribbons will wave around, as the airflow has been disturbed.

Anemometer

An anemometer measures wind speed. The Wright brothers used a handheld anemometer to estimate wind speed when they tested their flying machines. You can make an anemometer to record wind speed near your home.

SUPPLIES

- egg carton
- scissors
- markers
- 2 long straws
- clear tape
- pencil with eraser end
- straight pin
- stopwatch or watch with a second hand

1 Cut out four separate egg cups from the carton. Make a design with the markers on one cup and set the cups to one side.

2 Make an X with the straws and tape the center of the X securely with clear tape.

3 Tape one egg cup to the end of each straw so they all face the same direction.

4 Push the pin through the straw X and into the eraser end of the pencil. The X needs to spin freely.

5 Take your anemometer outside on a windy day. Push the sharp end of the pencil into the ground.

6 The egg cup with the design is your starting point. Using a stopwatch, count how many times it goes by in one minute. This number tells you the speed of the wind. For example, two revolutions per minute could mean that the wind speed is 2 miles per hour (3 kilometers).

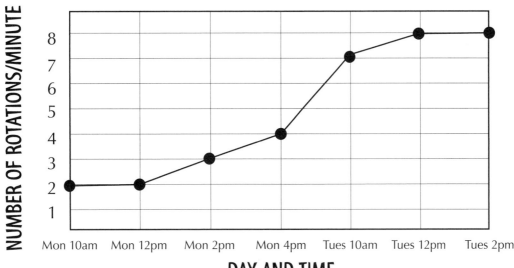

THINGS TO TRY: Record your information on a line graph listing date, time, and number of rotations. Create your line graph online at nces.ed.gov/nceskids/createagraph/default.aspx. What do you think your line graph will tell you about the wind conditions near your home?

Record the wind speeds at different times of the day. Record the wind speeds in different locations near your home, in the open and in more protected areas.

THINGS TO THINK ABOUT: Why did the Wright brothers need to know wind speed? How could they have used this information? What effect does location have on wind speed?

Then & Now

THEN: In 1911, Harriet Quimby became the first woman to get a pilot's license in the United States.

NOW: Over 42,000 women in the United States have pilot certificates.

Taketombo

Aviators such as the Wright brothers played with toy helicopters as children. You can make your own with paper. This toy helicopter is called a taketombo or bamboo dragonfly. The top of a taketombo resembles a propeller. **This activity uses a hot glue gun, so ask an adult to help.**

1 Measure and cut out a rectangle from your cardstock ½ x 5 inches (1 x 13 centimeters). Cut off the corners for the propeller. Decorate the propeller with colored pencils or markers.

2 Cut your skewer to 6½ inches long (16½ centimeters). Place a drop of hot glue in the center of one side of the propeller. Push the flat end of the bamboo skewer into the glue until the glue cools.

3 Hold the taketombo with the skewer between your palms and spin it rapidly before letting go. Then watch it fly!

THINGS TO TRY: Using a stopwatch, time how long it takes your taketombo to reach the ground from various heights. Make the propeller longer or wider. Predict what you think will happen and test it.

WHAT'S HAPPENING? As your taketombo falls, air is pushing up against the propeller. A longer or wider propeller will increase the surface area. This means there will be more air resistance and the taketombo will fall more slowly.

SUPPLIES

- thin bamboo skewer
- scissors
- cardstock or file folder
- pencil
- ruler
- scissors
- colored pencils or markers
- hot glue

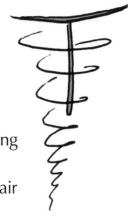

44

Golden Age of Flight

The 1920s and '30s are often called the Golden Age of Flight because it was an exciting time in aviation history. Passenger planes like you might travel on today didn't exist yet. People found airplanes simply amazing.

• •

Newspaper headlines announced record-setting flights and made celebrities out of pilots. There were many **daredevil** pilots in the news. One of these pilots, Lincoln Beachey, flew his biplane over Niagara Falls, under the steel arches of the Falls View Bridge. And he claimed to have done it with his eyes closed because of the water spray!

In the 1920s, **barnstorming** was a popular form of entertainment. A barnstormer was the name for a pilot who performed daredevil stunts, often above fields. Many barnstormers had been pilots in World War I. When the war ended, the United States had extra biplanes that pilots could buy for just $200.

Barnstormers shocked crowds with aerial stunts. There were wing walkers, people who leapt from plane to plane, and pilots who hung from ladders during flight. Many barnstormers were women. Crowds flocked to see Blanche Stuart Scott, the first female stunt flyer, who performed upside-down tricks 4,000 feet up in the air (1,214 meters).

Florence Lowe "Pancho" Barnes invited a member of the audience for a ride in her plane. When the plane was in flight, she pushed the passenger out, but not without first pulling the cord to open the parachute! Other famous pilots included Ruth Law, who formed a flying circus, and Roscoe Turner, who opened a flight school during World War II. Bessie Coleman was famous as the first licensed African American female pilot.

ELIZABETH "BESSIE" COLEMAN

Bessie Coleman became fascinated with flight after reading about aviation and hearing about it from her brother John, who had served in World War I. Coleman wanted to go to flight school. No American flight school would take her because she was African American and a woman, so she went to flight school in France. She got her pilot's license in 1921 and later become a barnstormer.

Coleman gave her first air show in the United States on September 3, 1922, in Garden City, New York. She became an instant celebrity and traveled across America encouraging other African Americans to fly. In 1995, the U.S. Postal Service designed a stamp honoring Coleman.

AIRMAIL

WORDS TO KNOW!

airmail: mail sent by air.

While aerial circuses were thrilling, there were everyday uses for airplanes too. On September 23, 1911, at the International Aviation Tournament in New York, people were invited to write postcards to go anywhere in the United States. They didn't know that a pilot named Earle Ovington would be taking those letters on the first official **airmail** flight in the United States. With a bag of mail between his legs, Ovington flew to the town of Mineola, a few miles away, where the mail was put on a train.

WORDS TO KNOW!

contact flying: navigating by watching for landmarks.

beacon: a machine that sent out radio waves to help pilots navigate.

In 1918, the Post Office began moving mail regularly by plane. In 1924, it took a train three days to deliver mail across the country. A plane could do it in 29 hours! From 1918 to 1926, the Post Office hired more than 200 pilots. Pilots relied on a simple compass and familiar landmarks such as buildings or railroads to find their way. This is called **contact flying**. Pilots also strapped a scrolling map to their legs, which they unrolled as they went.

By the 1920s, the Post Office was flying the mail at night, but it was very dangerous. Post Office staff and farmers lit large fires along the route to guide the pilots. By 1923, there were some lighted landing fields, and 289 **beacons** guided pilots across the United States.

JUST FOR LAUGHS

Why was the witch late for her reunion?
Because she missed her fright!

DARING FLIGHTS

People are always looking for a new challenge. On June 15, 1919, British aviator John Alcock and **navigator** Arthur Whitten-Brown made the first nonstop flight across the Atlantic Ocean from Newfoundland, Canada, to Ireland.

WORDS TO KNOW!

navigator: a person in charge of choosing a travel route.

That same year, a prize of $25,000 was offered to the first aviator who could fly nonstop between New York and Paris. Eight years later, 25-year-old airmail pilot Charles Lindbergh decided to try. On May 20, 1927, Lindbergh took to the air in his Ryan monoplane named *Spirit of St. Louis*. It took him 33 hours to complete the 3,600-mile journey (5,794 kilometers). At one point in flight, Lindbergh fell asleep! Luckily, he woke up as his plane began a diving roll. Millions welcomed him home with a parade in New York City.

DID YOU KNOW?

Long-distance flights in the 1920s were difficult. Pilots relied on the sun, a compass, and landmarks such as rivers to guide them. But this didn't work for pilots flying over deserts in the Middle East. So the British Royal Air Force dug a channel 2 yards wide (1.8 meters) and 310 miles long (500 kilometers) through the deserts of Iraq. Pilots following this channel referred to it as "flying the furrow."

AMELIA EARHART

Female pilots were also setting records in the 1920s and '30s. One of the best known was Amelia Earhart. Earhart's first flight was in California in 1920. Afterward, she said, "As soon as I left the ground, I knew I myself had to fly." By 1922, Earhart had her pilot's license and her name in the record books for setting the women's altitude record when she flew at 14,000 feet (4,267 meters).

On June 17, 1928, Earhart and pilots Wilmer Stultz and Louis Gordon set off from Newfoundland to Wales. Earhart did not take the controls until the final short flight from Wales to Southampton, England. But the flight brought her international fame. She became the first woman to fly across the Atlantic as a passenger.

WORDS TO KNOW!

orbit: the path an object in space takes around another object.

INSPIRED INVENTION

While the 1900s saw the world's first passenger airliner, in 2013 it might be possible to shoot up into **orbit** and fly around Earth in only a few hours. As of the summer of 2012, 529 people had paid deposits for the $200,000 ticket aboard *SpaceShipTwo* run by Virgin Galactic.

...COAST GUARD, PLEASE RESPOND...

WORDS TO KNOW!

equator: an imaginary line around the earth halfway between the North and South Poles.

Then & Now

Then: The first commercial airline in the United States was the St. Petersburg Tampa Airboat Line, which flew 172 flights in 4 months.

Now: In the 10-year period from 2002 to 2011, American Airlines flew almost 8 million flights.

A few years later, in 1932, Earhart flew her own plane across the Atlantic Ocean. Three years later, she became the first person to fly alone from Hawaii to the U.S. mainland. But Earhart's biggest world record attempt was yet to come.

In 1937, Earhart tried to fly around the world with Fred Noonan as her navigator. Her route mainly followed the **equator**. They flew over long stretches of water between islands in the Pacific Ocean. On July 2, Earhart and Noonan took off on the longest stretch of their journey. They lost radio contact with the ship that was trailing them and it was too cloudy to navigate using the stars. They missed their landing to get more fuel. Earhart and Noonan were never found. On July 19, 1937, after a huge search, they were declared lost at sea. Even now, people still search for and wonder what happened to Amelia Earhart.

RECORD BREAKER

On October 14, 1947, a World War II **combat** pilot named Charles "Chuck" Yeager was at the controls of a new plane. Engineers designed the Bell X-1 to see if a pilot and a plane could fly faster than the speed of sound. Yeager became the first person to break the **sound barrier** by flying 769 miles per hour (1,237 kilometers per hour). He shattered his record in 1952 by flying almost twice the speed of sound!

WORDS TO KNOW!

combat: used in fighting.

sound barrier: the sharp increase in drag as an aircraft approaches the speed of sound.

subsonic: flying at 350 to 750 miles per hour (563 to 1,207 kilometers per hour).

supersonic: flying at 760 to 3,500 miles per hour (1,223 to 5,632 kilometers per hour).

The sound barrier isn't a real obstacle like a wall. It is the point when an airplane travels faster than sound or when a plane moves from **subsonic** to **supersonic** speed. Sound travels at about 680 miles per hour (1,100 kilometers per hour) at an altitude of 40,000 feet (12,192 meters). When the sound barrier is broken, it makes a sonic boom that sounds like thunder.

BOOM

TUSKEGEE AIRMEN

On July 18, 1941, the U.S. Air Force began a program to train African American airmen in Tuskegee, Alabama. Before this time, African Americans had not been allowed to fly. But this changed for the men who trained at the Tuskegee Army Air Field. They became the first African Americans to fly combat aircraft. Some became navigators, mechanics, and control tower operators. Others became pilots. Between 1941 and 1945, 966 African American men graduated as pilots.

WORDS TO KNOW!

civilian: someone not in the military.

PEARL HARBOR

On December 7, 1941, Japan bombed the U.S. naval base in Pearl Harbor on the island of Hawaii. Americans prepared for more attacks. Over 600,000 American **civilians** worked as aircraft spotters. Spotters could recognize the shapes of U.S. and enemy planes and tell them apart. A seven-year-old spotter based in New Jersey was one of the youngest. His father bragged that his son could spot and identify planes much quicker than the older folk.

Water Compass

In the 1920s and '30s, pilots had simple equipment such as a bubble of liquid to help them keep a plane's wings level and a compass for direction. Today, most airplanes use ground-based radio transmitters to help pilots navigate. This activity will help you find your way with a compass.

1 Hold the magnet in one hand and the needle in the other. Rub the needle across the surface of the magnet, 15–20 times, to magnetize it.

2 Fill the bowl with water and place it on a level surface. Put the cap, bottom side up, in the water.

3 Carefully place your magnetized needle on top of the cap. Watch what happens.

WHAT IS HAPPENING? The needle on your compass should turn slowly north. You can use this point to figure out other directions.

American children built over 500,000 model airplanes during World War II to help train navy, army, and civilian spotters.

DID YOU KNOW?

Morse Code

Morse Code was invented by Samuel Morse in the mid-1830s. It used a system of short and long sounds to send a message with a telegraph. You and a friend are going to try sending secret messages to each other using Morse Code.

- paper and pencils

1 Write a short message down first and then translate it into Morse Code. Send it to your friend.

2 See if you can figure out your friend's response.

3 Now use a pencil to tap out the message in Morse Code. A dash is a long pause and a dot is a quick tap.

4 Your friend can answer the message using another pencil.

MORSE CODE

A . –	H	O – – –	V . . . –	2 . . – – –	9 – – – – .
B – – . . .	I . .	P . – – .	W . – –	3 . . . – –	**Full Stop**
C – . – .	J . – – –	Q – – . –	X – . . –	4 . . . . –	. – . – . –
D – . .	K – . –	R . – .	Y – . – –	5	**Comma**
E .	L . – . .	S . . .	Z – – . .	6 –	– – . . – –
F . . – .	M – –	T –	0 – – – – –	7 – – . . .	**Question**
G – – .	N – .	U . . –	1 . – – – –	8 – – – . .	. . – – . .

Design a Postcard

Long before the invention of the Internet, stagecoaches, horses, ships, and trains carried letters across North America. Once airplanes began delivering the mail, it was easier to stay in touch across long distances. You are going to design a postcard and mail it. Track how long it takes to arrive!

1 Measure a rectangle on the poster board that is 3¾ inches tall and 5½ inches wide (9½ by 14 centimeters). Cut it out. On one side, draw a line from top to bottom a little more than halfway from the left side.

2 Write the address of the person you are sending the postcard to on the right side. Put your return address just above it.

3 Write your message on the left side. Then decorate the blank side of the postcard however you want.

4 Bring your postcard to a post office, buy a stamp, put it on the back, and mail it. Make a note of when you sent the postcard and ask the recipient when it arrives so you can track how long it takes.

THINGS TO TRY: Send postcards to people in different parts of the country. Does it take longer to arrive at a location farther away? How much longer? How long does it take to mail overseas? How much more does it cost? Why?

Modern Aircraft

Do you think you would have been brave enough to be one of the first passengers ever to fly across the country? In July 1929, passengers on Transcontinental Air Transport traveled from New York to Los Angeles in two days. They flew on planes during the day and rode on trains at night because night flying was too dangerous.

By the 1930s, modern passenger airliners like the Boeing 247D were larger and more advanced with room for three crew and 10 passengers. It took 20 hours and seven stops for the 247D to travel between New York and Los Angeles!

Boeing kept up their innovation with its B314, known as the Clipper. In the late 1930s when there weren't many airports, most flights that crossed oceans were made on this plane. Also known as the Flying Boat, the Clipper could land on water.

During World War II, only warplanes traveled across the Atlantic to Europe. Most stopped in Gander, Newfoundland, for refueling and maintenance. By the end of the war, more than 20,000 combat aircraft built in North America had flown from Gander across the Atlantic Ocean.

After the war, many airlines offered air service to passengers on fast jet planes. These modern planes were larger, faster, and much more comfortable than early passenger aircraft.

INSPIRED INVENTION

NASA, Boeing, and Gulfstream are working together to build a supersonic jet capable of flying from London, England, to Sydney, Australia, in only four hours. It will travel at 2,500 miles per hour (4,023 kilometers per hour)!

A new Boeing 747, like one you might fly on today, can get to most parts of the United States in a few hours. This massive plane's tail is the size of a six-story building. One wing has an area large enough to hold 45 cars. No wonder more than 3 billion people have flown on the world's 747 fleet. That's equal to almost half of the world's population!

JUST FOR LAUGHS

What do airplanes do in their spare time?
They hang out!

Today's planes have computer-assisted flight controls that help pilots fly planes. In the future, all aircraft may connect to the Airborne Internet. This does not mean pilots will be surfing the Internet while they fly. Instead, it will make air travel even safer by making it easier to track planes from the ground. Pilots will be able to check traffic in the air around them.

PARTS OF AN AIRPLANE

Even with all these advances, modern airplanes still have the same basic parts as early planes. On every plane, you'll find the **fuselage**, wings, tail assembly, and engines.

TAIL ASSEMBLY

WING

ENGINE

FUSELAGE

When you fly on a plane, you sit in the fuselage. It's the tube-shaped body of the aircraft. Its shape is aerodynamic. Air flows smoothly around it to decrease drag. The pilot and copilots sit in the nose of the fuselage in the cockpit. The cockpit is filled with the buttons, lights, levers, controls, and display instruments needed for flying.

At the end of the fuselage, a number of pieces extend off the back of the plane. Together, these are called the tail assembly. The **vertical stabilizer**, or the fin, sticks up into the air and keeps the plane from rocking side to side. Its movable rudder helps steer the plane left or right. The **horizontal stabilizers** that come off each side keep the plane from rocking up and down. Their elevator flaps control up and down motions.

WORDS TO KNOW!

fuselage: the body of a plane.

vertical stabilizer: the part of the tail that extends up into the air.

horizontal stabilizer: a part of the tail that extends off to the sides.

Modern Aircraft

The wings are attached to the middle of the fuselage. They are curved on top so the plane can lift off the ground. Flaps and **ailerons** can be raised up or lowered down below the wing. To increase lift on takeoff, a pilot may keep the flaps flat, or even lower them

a little. For landing, pilots lower to "full flaps," which increases drag and slows down the plane. The ailerons are flaps near

the tip of each wing that move in opposite directions. When one moves up, the other moves down. This helps the plane make a right or left turn.

A plane's power comes from the forward thrust of its engines. Some planes use engines with

propellers on the front that pull the craft through the air. Others have jets under their wings.

The fastest commercial airliner was the Concorde, built by Britain and France. It carried passengers from London to New York in just three hours! Cruising at 1,354 miles per hour (2,179 kilometers per hour), it was the only passenger jet to fly above the speed of sound. After 24 years of flying, the Concorde had a deadly crash in July 2000 and has not flown since.

DID YOU KNOW?

HOW A JET ENGINE WORKS

It's always exciting to see a plane lift off the ground. You probably know that most planes today use a jet engine to thrust it forward.

A jet engine looks like a tube with a fan in the front. The fan sucks in air. Inside the engine, a **compressor** squeezes the air to raise the air pressure. Then the air is mixed with fuel and lit with an electric spark. The heated gases blast out the back of the engine. The blast generates the thrust that pushes the airplane forward.

The first plane to fly using only a jet engine was the Heinkel He 178, built in 1939. It reached speeds of 375 miles per hour (598 kilometers per hour). Now the fastest jet on record is the Lockheed SR-71 Blackbird Strategic Reconnaissance Jet. It has flown as fast as 2,500 miles per hour (4,022 kilometers per hour)!

WORDS TO KNOW!

compressor: a machine that supplies air at increased pressure.

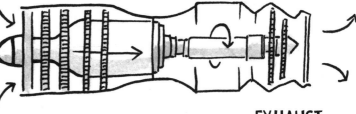

INTAKE   COMBUSTION

EXHAUST

The turbojet, turbofan, turboprop, turboshaft, and ramjet are all types of jet engines.

DID YOU KNOW?

WORKING PLANES

All of the hundreds of different aircraft are designed for a specific purpose. Some deliver packages and cargo, while others move people from place to place. Crop dusters spray pesticides so bugs don't eat crops, and military planes are used for defense and **surveillance**. Below are just a few examples of the different jobs airplanes do today.

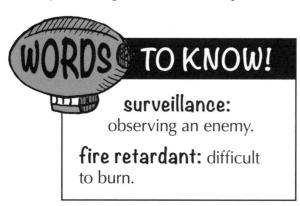

WORDS TO KNOW!

surveillance: observing an enemy.

fire retardant: difficult to burn.

AERIAL FIREFIGHTING: During the 1950s, surplus World War II military planes were turned into air tankers. Air tankers carry **fire retardant** chemicals or water to fight fire from the air. While flying the Canadair CL-415, the pilot can open the plane's belly doors to drop 1,621 gallons of water or chemicals onto a fire (6,137 liters). Then the plane swoops down over a lake and the pilot refills its tanks in just over 10 seconds!

Then & Now

Then: In 1952, the first jet airliner, named the Comet, took to the skies at a cruising speed of 490 miles per hour (789 kilometers per hour) with room for 44 passengers.

Now: The Boeing 747 cruises at 567 miles per hour (913 kilometers per hour) and can carry up to 345 people.

HOSPITAL PLANES: Hospital planes fly to remote areas of the world. One example is the Orbis, the only flying eye hospital in the world. The plane and its volunteer crew travel around the globe to perform sight-saving treatments in developing nations. The Orbis looks like a regular DC-10, but inside it has been re-designed into a state-of-the-art eye hospital. It has an operating room, a laser treatment facility, and a high-tech classroom.

PRESIDENTIAL PLANES: In 1943, Franklin Roosevelt became the first president in office to travel by air when he boarded a 314 Clipper to Casablanca. For over 20 years, presidents flew on propeller aircraft. But in 1962, President John F. Kennedy became the first president to fly in a customized Boeing 707. Over the years, other types of aircraft have been used.

Former President Nixon's Air Force One plane, which was used by presidents for almost 30 years until 2001, is now on display at the Ronald Reagan Presidential Library.

DID YOU KNOW?

Currently, the President of the United Sates flies on one of two customized Boeing 747-200B series planes kept at Andrews Air Force Base in Maryland. The planes are blue and white with an American flag, the Seal of the President, and the words "United States of America" in huge letters painted on the side.

The president's plane is called Air Force One. Air Force One is the **call sign** for any aircraft carrying the president. A call sign is used in aviation to identify an aircraft or a pilot over a radio. Air Force One is more than just an

WORDS TO KNOW!

call sign: a unique name given to an aircraft or pilot as identification.

airplane—it's a mobile White House. On board, its two kitchens are large enough to be used to make meals for 100 people. It has an office and chambers for the president and the first lady, a conference room, and rooms for the press and the secret service.

MODERN HELICOPTERS

If you were offered a ride in a whirly bird, a chopper, or an eggbeater, would you know it meant a helicopter? In the early 1900s, many inventions had whirling wings. Some made it off the ground but none was capable of controlled flight until a Spaniard named Juan de la Cierva created the Autogiro in 1923.

versatile: able to be used in lots of ways.

troops: soldiers.

The Autogiro had a propeller on the front that pulled it through the air and rotating blades on top for lift. During the 1930s, many people thought everyone in the future would have an Autogiro. Do you know anyone who has a helicopter? Very few people own their own, but a helicopter is a **versatile** machine. They can hover, go forward and backward, move side to side, and rotate. They can even take off and land in a vertical position so they don't need a runway.

Because helicopters only need an area the size of a school bus, they have more uses than airplanes. They are used for search and rescue, as air taxis, in firefighting and law enforcement, and for covering news stories. They can deliver supplies and **troops** in tight locations during war and serve as air ambulances.

The Sikorsky CH-53E Super Stallion is the largest and heaviest helicopter used by the U.S. military. It can transport 55 troops or carry 30,000 pounds of cargo inside (13,607 kilograms), or 36,000 pounds outside (16,329 kilograms).

JUST FOR LAUGHS

Who un-invented the airplane?
The Wrong brothers!

Paper Airplane

You may not be an aircraft engineer yet, but paper airplanes are a great way to learn how airplanes fly.

1 Cut your paper in half the short way and put one half to the side.

2 Fold the piece you are using in half lengthwise, then unfold.

3 Fold down the top corners so they meet each other at the centerline and re-fold the paper in half.

4 To make the wings, fold each side so it touches the middle fold.

5 Using a second sheet of paper, make another plane with a different wing shape. Also try adding weights like paper clips. Leave the other airplane as is, so you can test them side by side.

THINGS TO TRY: Using a stopwatch, time how long each plane stays in the air. Using a measuring tape, see how far each plane travels. Make a plane from a heavier paper such as a file folder, and one from lighter paper such as newsprint. Predict what will happen before you launch your aircrafts. Make graphs of your results.

SUPPLIES

- scissors
- construction paper
- paper clips
- stopwatch or a watch with a second hand
- measuring tape
- file folder
- newsprint
- graph paper and pencil

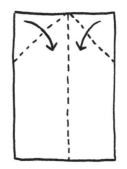

Windsock

A windsock is a type of kite used at airports. It shows pilots the direction the wind is blowing. After you make your windsock, you will always know the wind's direction.

SUPPLIES

- 1 yard of fabric (91 centimeters)
- fabric scissors
- fabric markers
- ruler
- sewing needle
- cotton thread
- 16-gauge wire or less
- needle nose pliers
- yarn or twine
- safety pins

1 Cut your fabric into a rectangle roughly 12 x 24 inches (30 x 60 centimeters) and decorate it with fabric markers.

2 Turn the fabric inside out and fold it in half. Sew the seam and one end.

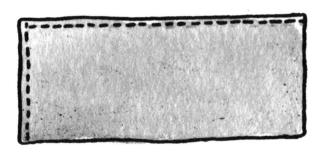

3 Fold over about ½ inch of the open end (1 centimeter) to make a casing for the wire. Sew the casing using long running stitches. When you are finished, pull the thread to scrunch the fabric. Do not tie a knot or remove the needle because you may need to adjust the material after you insert the wire.

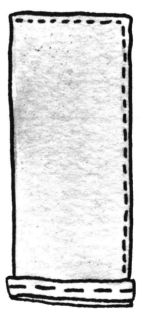

4 Cut a 15-inch piece of wire (38 centimeters) and make a loop on one end. Starting with the loop, push the wire through the casing. When the wire is all the way through, twist the ends together. Adjust your fabric and knot the thread.

5 Cut a piece of yarn 24-inches long (62 centimeters). Safety pin or sew the yarn to opposite sides of the loop.

6 Loop the yarn around a pole or a sturdy stick so it stays on. On a windy day, can you tell which direction the wind is blowing?

WHAT'S HAPPENING? As the wind blows, the windsock fills with air. This causes the windsock to point in that direction.

THINGS TO THINK ABOUT: How does the windsock move in the wind? Why would pilots be taught to land into the wind and take off with the wind behind them?

JUST FOR LAUGHS

Why is it always windy at baseball games?
Because of all the fans!

Call Sign

Did you know that pilots send messages in a special language? It's called the International Phonetic Alphabet. With everyone using the same alphabet, it's easier to communicate. And no one will think you said E when you really said D. You are going to use the alphabet to make your own call sign.

1 Write down your favorite food, sport, and color.

2 Take the first letter from each word and find the corresponding word in the aviator's alphabet. So pizza, football, and blue would be PFB. You would say papa foxtrot bravo.

PHONETIC ALPHABET

A Alpha	**H** Hotel	**O** Oscar	**V** Victor
B Bravo	**I** India	**P** Papa	**W** Whiskey
C Charlie	**J** Juliet	**Q** Quebec	**X** X ray
D Delta	**K** Kilo	**R** Romeo	**Y** Yankee
E Echo	**L** Lima	**S** Sierra	**Z** Zulu
F Foxtrot	**M** Mike	**T** Tango	
G Golf	**N** November	**U** Uniform	

The Space Age

For thousands of years people have dreamed of more than just flight on Earth. People have also dreamed of flight among the stars. An ancient Chinese legend tells of a local official named Wan Hu who dreamed of flying into space. One day, he tied 47 gunpowder rockets to the base of a chair. His 47 assistants lit the rocket fuses. There was a huge explosion. When the smoke cleared, Wan Hu was gone. No one knows if Wan Hu made it into space but today rockets are used to travel into space.

• •

Like many inventions, it took the ideas, designs, and work of many people over many years to build rockets. These rockets send people into space, allow them to walk on the moon, and bring them back safely. Are you surprised to find out that rockets may have started as a toy?

71

WORDS TO KNOW!

Sir Isaac Newton: a British scientist who lived in the 1600s and studied motion and gravity.

rocketry: the study of rocket design and use.

In 400 BCE, a Greek man named Archytas built a wooden pigeon, suspended it with a wire, and used steam to make it fly. Around the first century CE, the Chinese learned to make explosive gunpowder. They stuffed the powder into hollow bamboo tubes and threw them on a fire. It is thought that some did not explode but took off like rockets. There are reports that in 1232 CE, the Chinese were seen attaching bamboo tubes filled with gunpowder to arrows. These fire arrow rockets were used to confuse enemy troops.

INSPIRED INVENTIONS

Juno is an unmanned rocket designed by NASA to explore Jupiter. NASA launched the sun-powered robotic explorer in 2011. It will take *Juno* five years to travel the 1.7 billion miles to Jupiter (2.7 billion kilometers).

In 1687, British scientists began to understand the science behind rockets. This is when **Sir Isaac Newton** wrote three laws explaining motion. His third law stated that for every action there is an equal and opposite reaction. This is the key idea behind **rocketry**. What happens when you let air out of a balloon? It goes flying forward, right? A rocket works the same way.

ROCKET INVENTIONS

By the nineteenth century, people all over the world were discovering many uses for rockets. Sailors attached rockets to harpoons in the 1800s to hunt whales. They carried the rockets on their shoulders and then fired the harpoon into the whale. They also used rockets to save lives at sea. A rope attached to a **Congreve rocket** could be sent from a ship's deck to a stranded person 1,000 feet away (305 meters)!

WORDS TO KNOW!

Congreve rocket: a rocket developed for warfare by Sir William Congreve in 1804.

By the twentieth century there were successful attempts to use rockets to deliver the mail in Europe, Southeast Asia, and North America. The United States Postal Service launched a missile carrying 3,000 letters from Virginia heading to Florida on June 8, 1959. It only took the missile 22 minutes to reach its destination in Florida where the mail was sorted and delivered.

JUST FOR LAUGHS

What do you get when you cross an airplane with a train?

A choo-choo plane!

EARLY ROCKET PIONEERS

Russian scientist Konstantin Tsiolkovsky was one of the first people to imagine the possibilities of space exploration. In 1898, he wrote the article *Investigating Space with Rocket Devices*, which contained many ideas used in modern spaceflight today.

On a Massachusetts farm in March 1926, American Robert H. Goddard successfully flew the first liquid-fueled rocket. This kind of rocket uses chemical fuels and gases like **oxygen**. Goddard's rocket climbed only 42 feet (12½ meters), but it was an important step in rocket design. Less than half a century later, a liquid-fueled rocket would carry the Apollo rockets to the moon. Until he died in 1945, Goddard made so many advances in rocketry that he is known as the father of modern rocketry.

WORDS TO KNOW!

oxygen: a gas in the air that animals and humans need to breathe to stay alive.

Across the Atlantic, a team of German engineers headed by Wernher von Braun were developing rockets too. During World War II, these rockets were used against cities including London, England. After the war, von Braun worked for the U.S. Army and at NASA. His team stacked two or more rockets on top of each another to gain more altitude and speed.

THE SPACE RACE

The space age began after World War II. The United States and the **Soviet Union** wanted to be the first to put a person on the moon. The Soviet Union led the Space Race with its launch of the first manmade **satellite**, *Sputnik I*, on October 4, 1957. About the size of a basketball, *Sputnik I* orbited Earth in 98 minutes.

WORDS TO KNOW!

Soviet Union: a country that existed from 1922 until 1991. Russia was part of the Soviet Union.

satellite: an object that orbits a larger object in space.

Two months later, *Sputnik II* was launched with the first live being ever to travel to outer space. The small dog named Laika orbited Earth for a few hours while a camera transmitted images of her back to Earth. Sadly, Laika died in space. Scientists did not yet know how to return her safely to Earth. After the launch of *Sputnik*, the United States created NASA and launched its own satellite, *Explorer I*.

In 1865, author Jules Verne wrote the science-fiction book *From the Earth to the Moon.* In the book three men are launched from Florida to the moon, which is exactly what the Apollo astronauts did in 1969.

DID YOU KNOW?

PEOPLE IN SPACE

On April 12, 1961, a Soviet **astronaut** named Yuri Gagarin became the first person to orbit Earth. His trip lasted 1 hour and 48 minutes. When his ship reentered Earth's **atmosphere**, Gagarin parachuted from the capsule safely to the ground. A month later, on May 5, 1961, it was America's turn. Alan Shephard Jr. lifted off in the *Freedom* spacecraft atop a seven-story rocket. Shephard made a **suborbital** flight lasting 15 minutes and 22 seconds before his capsule returned to Earth and landed in the Atlantic Ocean.

Days after Shepherd's flight, President Kennedy challenged America. Before the end of the decade, he wanted to send an American astronaut to the moon and return him safely. NASA got right to work.

WORDS TO KNOW!

astronaut: a person who travels or works in space.

atmosphere: the blanket of air surrounding Earth.

suborbital: an aircraft that goes higher and faster than a plane but not into space.

module: a part of a space vehicle that can work on its own.

THE APOLLO PROGRAM

The Apollo Program was the name given by NASA to its efforts to explore the moon. The 11th mission in this series lifted off on July 16, 1969, for a three-day journey to the moon. Aboard were three astronauts: Neil Armstrong, Edwin "Buzz" Aldrin, and Michael Collins. Their ship, the *Apollo 1*, was made up of three **modules**.

THE COMMAND MODULE: The command module was manned by astronaut Michael Collins and stayed in orbit around the moon.

THE SERVICE MODULE: The service module, named *Columbia*, contained the fuel and power equipment.

WORDS TO KNOW!

lunar: relating to a moon or a vehicle used to travel to a moon.

THE LUNAR MODULE: Traveling in the **lunar** module *Eagle*, Neil Armstrong and Buzz Aldrin became America's first astronauts on the moon. They landed on July 20, 1969.

Eagle had a pressurized compartment for the crew and carried equipment to explore the lunar surface. Armstrong declared, "That's one small step for man, one giant leap for mankind." *Eagle* was abandoned in space, but *Columbia* is on display at the Smithsonian National Air and Space Museum in Washington, D.C.

SPACE SHUTTLE

On April 12, 1981, the first shuttle *Columbia* blasted into space from Cape Canaveral, Florida. It was the world's first reusable spacecraft. The Space Shuttle would be in service for 30 years. Dr. Sally K. Ride's flight on the *Columbia* in June 1983 made her the first American woman to fly in space. Guion S. Bluford Jr.'s flight in August 1983 made him the first African American astronaut in space.

WORDS TO KNOW!

orbiter: the vessel of the Space Shuttle that carried the crew.

The Space Shuttle's **orbiter**, rocket boosters, and fuel tank allowed it to be launched like a rocket, orbit like a spacecraft, and land as a glider. The orbiter looked like a large, white space airplane. It is where the astronauts worked, slept, ate, and conducted experiments. The orbiter was the only part of the shuttle that went into orbit.

Attached to the orbiter were wings shaped like triangles with the tips cut off, called delta wings. Regular airplane-shaped wings wouldn't provide the shuttle with enough lift at high speeds and altitudes.

FUEL TANK

ROCKET BOOSTERS

ORBITER

USA

The two rocket boosters provided energy to lift the shuttle and blast it into space. Two minutes after liftoff, they dropped off and parachuted into the ocean to be recovered and reused. For the next six minutes, the liquid fuel in the orange fuel tank on the outside of the shuttle powered the main engines. That tank then dropped off and the shuttle and crew were in orbit.

Shuttle astronauts collected samples, ran science experiments, tested equipment, and repaired spacecraft like the Hubble Space Telescope. Shuttle crews also helped build the *International Space Station*, the largest structure in space.

WORDS TO KNOW!

International Space Station: an artificial satellite on which astronauts have been living, conducting tests, and studying space for more than 11 years.

deep space: beyond the orbit of the moon.

Every shuttle mission is risky, and both the *Challenger* and *Columbia* shuttles crashed. In 2011, the Space Shuttle program saw its last mission with the orbiter *Atlantis*.

SPACE LAUNCH SYSTEM

NASA is at work on its next rocket, the Space Launch System (SLS). When completed it will be the most powerful rocket in history and will send astronauts farther into space than ever before! The SLS may even allow astronauts to explore Earth's asteroids and eventually Mars. It is being designed to support a crew of six astronauts for six months on **deep space** missions.

Rocket

Here's a quick and easy way to create your own rocket that you can even power.

1 Paint the body of your paper towel tube and let it dry.

2 On the construction paper, sketch two fins. Cut out the fins and tape them to the sides of the rocket.

3 Cut out a circle slightly larger than the tube opening for the nose cone. Make a slit from the edge of the circle to the center. Fold the circle by overlapping the edges to form a cone and tape it together.

4 Tape the nose cone to the body and paint and decorate your complete rocket.

SUPPLIES

- paper towel tube
- paint
- paint brush
- construction paper
- pencil
- scissors
- clear tape
- markers, stickers, any other decorations

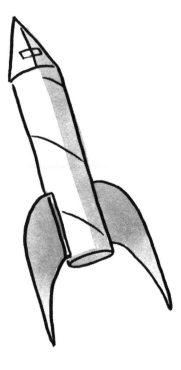

Then & Now

THEN: The Space Shuttle could carry the equivalent of five elephants or 65,000 pounds of cargo (29,482 kilograms).

NOW: The new SLS will be able to carry the equivalent of 22 elephants or 286,000 pounds of cargo (12,700 kilograms).

Power Rocket

Now add power to your rocket and watch it blast off!

1 Tape a straw to one side of your rocket.

2 Stretch a balloon several times in different directions. This will make it easier to inflate. Insert the balloon into the rocket tube, inflate the balloon, and tie it shut.

3 Attach a long piece of yarn or string to a doorknob. Thread the remaining string through the straw on the side of your rocket. The nose of your rocket must be pointing toward the door.

SUPPLIES

- drinking straw
- clear tape
- long balloon
- yarn or string
- scissors
- a doorknob
- a chair

4 Tie the end of the string to a chair positioned a few feet away (about 1 meter).

5 Bring the rocket down to the chair end. This is going to be the launching site.

6 Predict what you think will happen when you cut the knot off the balloon. Now try it and see if you were right!

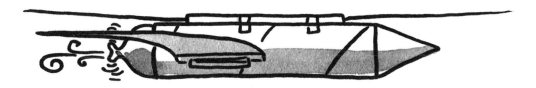

THINGS TO TRY: Try filling the balloon with less air. Try taping or tying the string from the floor to the ceiling. How far can your rocket go with its balloon fuel pack?

Hypersonic Vehicle

Hypersonic vehicles like the Space Shuttle can travel more than five times the speed of sound. The shuttle used special materials to keep the instruments and people on board safe from the heat of reentry. Currently, the fastest aircraft on Earth is the Falcon Hypersonic Test Vehicle, which is capable of flying at 20 times the speed of sound. Now imagine that you are a NASA spacecraft engineer. Design your own spacecraft using your imagination and what you've learned about forces and aerodynamic shapes. What will your hypersonic spacecraft look like and how will it fly?

SUPPLIES

- paper
- pencil and crayons
- assorted boxes and containers
- tape
- glue

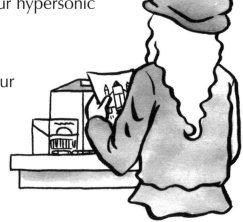

THINGS TO THINK ABOUT: How will your vehicle withstand high temperatures? How will your vehicle launch or land? How many occupants will it accommodate? How will your vehicle maneuver?

Then & Now

Then: In the first century CE, Hero, a man from Greece, powered a rocket-like device called an Aeolipile using steam to make a brass ball spin.

Now: Rockets are giant vehicles capable of traveling into outer space using liquid fuels such as oxygen.

Target Practice

It is not easy to set a course for Mars or any other planet or moon in our solar system. Not only is the spacecraft moving, but so is the object in space. In order to save fuel, the spacecraft is aimed where the planet or moon should be when the rocket is ready to land. In this game, you are going to discover how hard it is to hit a moving target.

SUPPLIES

- an even-numbered group of friends
- 2 pails
- adult helpers
- 2 lengths of rope
- 2 tennis balls

1 Divide your friends into two groups of even numbers.

2 Tie a length of rope to each pail and ask an adult to tie the other end to a tree branch or a play structure. The two pails should be far enough apart so they don't hit each other when they are swinging.

3 The adults should pull the pails back to start them swinging. Each team member has one chance to throw the ball into the pail. If the ball goes in, that person sits down. If it misses, he or she goes to the back of the line to try again. In between each turn, the adults keep the pails moving.

4 The first team to have all its members throw the ball into the moving target and be seated wins.

83

Glossary

aerodynamic: having a shape that reduces the amount of drag on something when it moves through the air.

aeronaut: a traveler in a flying craft.

aeronautics: the science of flight.

aileron: a flap on the end of each wing of an airplane.

air pressure: the force of air on something.

airmail: mail sent by air.

altitude: height above sea level.

American Civil War: a war fought from 1861 to 1865 between the 11 states that formed the Confederacy and the 25 Union states supported by the federal government.

anatomy: the structure of a living thing.

ancestor: a person who lived before you.

anemometer: a device used to measure wind speed.

astronaut: a person who travels or works in space.

atmosphere: the blanket of air surrounding Earth.

aviation: everything having to do with flight.

aviator: a pilot.

barnstorming: performing daring tricks in a plane.

BCE: put after a date, BCE stands for Before Common Era and counts down to zero. CE stands for Common Era and counts up from zero. These non-religious terms correspond to BC and AD.

beacon: a machine that sent out radio waves to help pilots navigate.

biplane: a plane with two pairs of wings, one above the other.

box-kite airplane: a kite with an engine and a tail added.

call sign: a unique name given to an aircraft or pilot as identification.

cargo: a load carried on a ship or aircraft.

catapult: a mechanical device that launches a glider or aircraft.

century: a period of 100 years.

civilian: someone not in the military.

combat: used in fighting.

commercial: operating as a business to earn money.

compressor: a machine that supplies air at increased pressure.

Congreve rocket: a rocket developed for warfare by Sir William Congreve in 1804.

contact flying: navigating by watching for landmarks.

Cretaceous Period: 144 to 65 million years ago.

daredevil: someone who enjoys doing dangerous things.

deep space: beyond the orbit of the moon.

Glossary

drag: the force pushing against an object as it moves through the air.

engineer: someone who uses science and math to design and build things.

English Channel: an arm of the Atlantic Ocean separating England from France.

equator: an imaginary line around the earth halfway between the North and South Poles.

fire retardant: difficult to burn.

force: a push or a pull.

fuselage: the body of a plane.

glide: to come in for a landing and to land without using engine power. Also, to move smoothly and effortlessly through the air or the water.

glider: an aircraft that can fly without an engine by riding air currents. It is towed up by an aircraft with an engine.

gravity: the pull of all objects toward the center of the earth.

hang glider: a piloted aircraft made of cloth that looks like a parachute or big kite.

horizontal stabilizer: a part of the tail that extends off to the sides.

hover: to float in the air without moving.

hydrogen: a gas that is lighter than air.

International Space Station: an artificial satellite on which astronauts have been living, conducting tests, and studying space for more than 11 years.

legend: a story about heroes from the past.

lift: an upward force.

lunar: relating to a moon or a vehicle used to travel to a moon.

mammal: a group of animals that includes humans, dogs, and mice. These animals have backbones, feed their young with milk, and are mostly covered with hair.

Medieval Era: A period of time between the fall of the Roman Empire and the Renaissance, roughly between 350 and 1450 CE. Also known as the Middle Ages.

module: a part of a space vehicle that can work on its own.

monoplane: an airplane with one set of wings.

myth: a story about make-believe creatures that people once believed were real.

NASA: the national organization in charge of the United States space program.

navigator: a person in charge of choosing a travel route.

orbit: the path an object in space takes around another object.

Glossary

orbiter: the vessel of the Space Shuttle that carried the crew.

oxygen: a gas in the air that animals and humans need to breathe to stay alive.

Palace of Versailles: the home of the French royal family who ruled from 1682 to 1789.

pioneer: to be the first to do or discover something.

prototype: a working model.

reptile: an animal covered with scales that crawls on its belly or on short legs. Snakes, turtles, and alligators are reptiles.

rocketry: the study of rocket design and use.

rudder: a fin-like device used to steer a vehicle through water or air.

sailplane: a piloted glider with aircraft parts, construction, and flight control systems, but no engine.

satellite: an object that orbits a larger object in space.

Sir Isaac Newton: a British scientist who lived in the 1600s and studied motion and gravity.

sound barrier: the sharp increase in drag as an aircraft approaches the speed of sound.

Soviet Union: a country that existed from 1922 until 1991. Russia was part of the Soviet Union.

species: a group of plants or animals that are the same.

steam engine: an engine powered by steam, first invented by James Watt in 1775.

suborbital: an aircraft that goes higher and faster than a plane but not into space.

subsonic: flying at 350 to 750 miles per hour (563 to 1,207 kilometers per hour).

supersonic: flying at 760 to 3,500 miles per hour (1,223 to 5,632 kilometers per hour).

surveillance: observing an enemy.

tandem wings: two full-sized wings, one in front of the other.

technology: tools, methods, or systems used to solve a problem or do work.

thrust: a force that pushes an object forward.

Triassic Period: 250 to 200 million years ago.

troops: soldiers.

versatile: able to be used in lots of ways.

vertical stabilizer: the part of the tail that extends up into the air.

World War I: a war centered in Europe that was fought from 1914 to 1918.

World War II: a war fought between most of the world's nations from 1939 to 1945.

Resources

BOOKS

Bell-Rehwoldt, Sherri. *Great World War II Projects You Can Build Yourself*, Nomad Press, 2006

Benoit, Peter. *The Hindenburg Disaster*, Children's Press, 2011

Borden, Louise and Mary Kay Krogen. *Fly High! The Story of Bessie Coleman*, Margaret K. McElderry Books, 2001

Bristow, David L. *Sky Sailors*, Farrar, Straus and Giroux, 2010

Brooks, Philip. *The Tuskegee Airmen*, Compass Point Books, 2005

Collicutt, Paul. *This Rocket*, Farrar, Straus and Giroux, 2005

Eason, Sarah. *How Does a Helicopter Work?* Gareth Stevens Publishing, 2010

Fleischman, John. *Black and White Airmen: Their True History*, Houghton Mifflin Books for Children, 2007

Freeman, Russell. *The Wright Brothers: How they invented the Airplane*, Holiday House, 1994

Fleming, Candace. *Amelia Lost: The Life and Disappearance of Amelia Earhart*, 2011

Graham, Ian. *The World of Flight*, Kingfisher, 2006

Graham, Ian. *You Wouldn't want to be a World War II Pilot*, Franklin Watts, 2009

Griffith, Victoria. *The Fabulous Flying Machine of Alberto Santos-Dumont*, Harry N. Abrams, 2011

Jennings, Terry J. *Planes, Gliders, Helicopters*, Kingfisher, 1993

Maynard, Christopher. *I Wonder Why Planes have Wings*, Kingfisher, 2012

Morano Kjelle, Marylou. *Explore Transportation! 25 Great Projects, Activities, Experiments*, Nomad Press, 2009

Moss, Marissa. *Sky High: The True Story of Maggie Gee*, Tricycle Press, 2009

Old, Wendie C. *The Wright Brothers: Inventors of the Airplane*, Enslow Publishers, Inc., 2000

Nahum, Andrew. *Flight*, DK Children, 2011

Rinard, Judith E. *Book of Flight: The Smithsonian National Air and Space Museum*, Firefly Books, 2007

Sandler, Martin W. *Flying over the U.S.A: Airplanes in America*, Oxford University Press, 2004

Tanaka, Shelley. *Amelia Earhart: The Legend of the Lost Aviator*, Abrams Books for Young Readers, 2008

Hardesty, Von. *Epic Adventure: Epic Flights*, Kingfisher, 2011

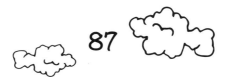

Resources

WEB SITES

American Experience: The Wright Stuff
www.pbs.org/wgbh/amex/wright

Aviation Pioneers: An Anthology
www.ctie.monash.edu.au/
hargrave/pioneers.html

Evolution of Flight www.flight100.org

Federal Aviation Administration
www.faa.gov/education/student_
resources/kids_corner

First Flight
firstflight.open.ac.uk/index.html

Flights of Inspiration: sln.fi.edu/flights

How Airplanes Work
www.howstuffworks.com/airplane/htm

Junior Flyer: www.juniorflyer.com

Milestones of Flight Gallery
www.nasm.si.edu/galleries/
gal100/gal100.htm

**United States Air Force
Museum Online Galleries**
www.wpafb.af.mil/museum

PBS Way Back History for Kids-Flight
pbskids.org/wayback/flight

**National Business
Aviation Association**
www.avkids.com

NASA Kids' Club
www.nasa.gov/audience/forkids/
kidsclub/flash/index.html

Women in Aviation Resource Center
www.women-in-aviation.com

MUSEUMS OF INTEREST

Aviation Enthusiasm Corner-Aviation Museum Locator
www.aero-web.org/museums/museums.htm

Airventure Museum www.airventuremuseum.org

National Museum of the United States Air Force
www.nationalmuseum.af.mil

The Museum of Flight and Aviation www.museumofflight.org

The New England Air Museum www.neam.org

The Intrepid Sea, Air, and Space Museum www.intrepidmuseum.org

Smithsonian National Air and Space Museum airandspace.si.edu

San Diego Air and Space Museum www.sandiegoairandspace.org

United States Army Aviation Museum www.armyavnmuseum.org

Index

Index